THE ROCK
CYCLE

by Rebecca E. Hirsch

Content Consultant
Dr. Kevin Theissen
Associate Professor and Chair
Department of Geology
University of Saint Thomas

Core Library

An Imprint of Abdo Publishing
www.abdopublishing.com

www.abdopublishing.com

Published by Abdo Publishing, a division of ABDO, PO Box 398166,
Minneapolis, Minnesota 55439. Copyright © 2015 by Abdo Consulting
Group, Inc. International copyrights reserved in all countries. No part of
this book may be reproduced in any form without written permission from
the publisher. Core Library™ is a trademark and logo of Abdo Publishing.

Printed in the United States of America, North Mankato, Minnesota
032014
092014

THIS BOOK CONTAINS
RECYCLED MATERIALS

Cover Photo: Thinkstock
Interior Photos: Thinkstock, 1, 4, 12, 29; Valeriya Repina/Thinkstock,
7; Shutterstock Images, 10, 15, 30, 45; Kenneth Keifer/Thinkstock, 17;
Webspark/Shutterstock Images, 18; Ted S. Warren/AP Images, 20; Filipe
Wiens/Thinkstock, 22; Gary Yim/Shutterstock Images, 25; David Woods/
Shutterstock Images, 27; Chris Gardiner/Thinkstock, 32; Alexander
Mustard/AP Images, 36; Daniel Prudek/Shutterstock Images, 39; Davis
McCardle/Thinkstock, 40; Albina Tiplyashina/Shutterstock Images, 42 (top);
Les Palenik/Shutterstock Images, 42 (bottom); Dan Schreiber/Shutterstock
Images, 43

Editor: Lauren Coss
Series Designer: Becky Daum

Library of Congress Control Number: 2014932350

Cataloging-in-Publication Data
Hirsch, E. Rebecca.
 The rock cycle / Rebecca E. Hirsch.
   p. cm. -- (Rocks and minerals)
Includes bibliographical references and index.
ISBN 978-1-62403-389-6
1. Petrology--Juvenile literature. 2. Geochemical cycles--Juvenile literature.
I. Title.
552--dc23

                                                          2014932350

CONTENTS

CHAPTER ONE

WHAT IS THE ROCK CYCLE?

The planet Earth is one huge rock. Wherever you live, you do not have to look far to find a rock. Rocks are the most common materials on Earth. Next time you take a walk outside, look around. What kinds of rocks do you see? Depending on where you live, you might see hills or mountains. You might see jagged cliffs or tiny grains of sand. You might see

Geologists have gathered important clues about Earth's history by studying the rock formations that make up the Grand Canyon in Arizona.

How You Use Rocks and Minerals

Americans use huge quantities of materials from the earth. Rocks forming sand, gravel, and cement make roads and sidewalks. Minerals such as iron, aluminum, and copper make wire, cars, metal buildings, and more. The mineral salt goes on your food and melts ice on roads and sidewalks in the winter.

rocks poking out of the soil or smooth pebbles at the bottom of a stream.

Rocks in Your World

Many of the objects we use every day come from rocks. Houses can be made of bricks and plaster, which both come from rocks. The glass in windows is made from quartz sand. Sidewalks and roads may be made of concrete. These aren't the only rocks we use. Rocks are even used as fuel to heat buildings, power cars, and generate electricity.

So what exactly is a rock? All rocks are made of minerals. These are naturally occurring solids. All minerals are made of one or more elements. A mineral is the same throughout. This means if you cut

Iron ore from rocks is used to make steel, which is used to make everything from paper clips to bridges.

a mineral into parts, all parts have exactly the same chemical makeup. Minerals include substances like aluminum, copper, gold, iron ore, nickel, and silver. The salt you sprinkle on your food is a mineral. So is the fluoride in your toothpaste.

Minerals are the building blocks of rocks. Rocks are made up of one or more minerals. Sometimes you can even see the different specks of minerals in a rock.

By studying the minerals in a certain rock, scientists can learn what kind of rock it is. For example, granite is made up of the minerals quartz and feldspar and may also contain bits of biotite. Some rocks are made of the remains of living things. Limestone is a rock that is often made of seashells. Coal is made of decayed plants.

Relying on Rocks

Humans have been using rocks for almost as long as we have been around. Early humans discovered that rocks could be made into tools. They used rocks as hammers and scrapers for skinning and butchering animals. Later, they attached rocks to sticks to make the first arrows and spears. This time in history is called the Stone Age. It began almost 3 million years ago and ended around 6000 BCE.

The Rock Cycle

How are living things and minerals turned into rocks? Think about a glass bottle or an aluminum can. When you are finished using a bottle or can, do you recycle it? Have you ever wondered what happens to the things you recycle? The old glass or can is melted down and made into something new.

Nature also recycles. Rocks are made, destroyed, and made again into something new. This process is called the rock cycle, and it has been going on for billions of years. The rock cycle sometimes happens quickly, right before your eyes. For example, when a volcano erupts, the molten rock cools and hardens into new rocks very quickly. When a jagged cliff crumbles, the old rock is broken into smaller rocks.

Other changes take millions of years. The changes may be hidden deep inside the earth. There, heat and pressure can change old rocks into new ones. Deep underground, small bits of rock are pressed together to form new rocks. Deep in the ocean, rocks slowly sink back into the earth.

During the rock cycle, different kinds of rocks form. When molten, or melted, rock cools and becomes solid, igneous rocks form. When bits of other rocks are worn away and then pressed together in layers, sedimentary rocks form. When rocks are squeezed and heated, they can transform

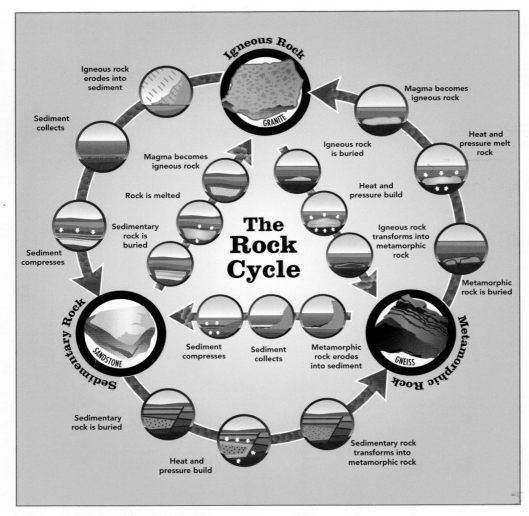

The Rock Cycle

This diagram shows the rock cycle. How does seeing the diagram help you better understand how rocks are made and recycled?

into metamorphic rocks. The rock cycle goes on and on. Rocks are made. Rocks are destroyed. They are recycled into new rocks. The cycle never stops.

Not all rocks come from Earth. Meteors can be rocks that come from outer space. This excerpt describes a meteor that exploded over the Russian town of Chelyabinsk in 2013:

> While Chelyabinsk did not exactly dodge a bullet on Feb. 15, the city was fortunate to be only grazed by it. "The people of Chelyabinsk were very lucky," Edward Lu, a former astronaut who now leads the B612 Foundation, a private initiative to detect similar asteroids, said at a Congressional hearing last week about the space threats.
>
> The Russian meteor—which, according to the latest estimates, was about 60 feet in diameter and came in undetected at roughly 42,000 miles an hour—was almost 15 miles high when it blew apart. There were no deaths, and most of the 1,500 injuries were from glass as windows shattered when a shock wave hit the city 88 seconds later.
>
> Source: Henry Fountain. "A Clearer View of the Space Bullet That Grazed Russia." New York Times. New York Times Company, March 25, 2013. Web. Accessed November 26, 2013.

What's the Big Idea?

Read this passage closely. What is one of the writer's main points about the rock from space? Pick out two details the writer uses to make this point. What can you tell about the effects of the meteor based on this article?

CHAPTER TWO

EARTH'S LAYERS

Understanding the rock cycle means understanding the layers that make up the earth. Let's take a journey to the center of the earth. Imagine you are trying to dig a deep hole to the center of the earth. At first, you dig through soil. But then your shovel hits solid rock. To go farther you will need special equipment, such as a jackhammer or a drill.

Underneath the soil lies Earth's crust, which is made of rock.

Suppose you had the equipment to dig very deep. How far could you go? People have tried to drill into the earth, but nobody has succeeded. You would need a hole nearly 4,000 miles (6,400 km) deep to get to the center of the earth. If you could drill all the way to the center, what would you find?

Earth's Crust

If you drilled a hole in your backyard, you would pass through solid rock for the first 25 miles (40 km) or so. This layer is called the earth's crust. The crust is the layer you touch every day. Even the ocean is part of the crust. There, the crust lies deep underwater. The crust is the only layer of Earth that people have been able to explore.

The Mantle

After passing through the crust, you would reach a layer called the mantle. The mantle makes up the next 1,800 miles (2,900 km) of Earth. At first, the mantle is hard, just like the crust. As you dig deeper, the mantle

Mountains and valleys are part of Earth's crust.

gets hotter and denser. The rocks are so hot that they flow. They are more flexible, just as road tar is squishy and more flexible on a hot day. Here and there, pockets of rock melt. They form magma, a hot liquid made of melted rock and gas bubbles.

The rocks in the mantle do not sit still. Hot rocks rise and cooler rocks sink, creating currents. These currents in the mantle stretch and squeeze the crust

15

Explosive Yellowstone

Yellowstone National Park is famous for wild animals and geysers that shoot steaming water high in the air. But visitors to Yellowstone may not know that they are actually standing in a huge volcano crater. Yellowstone's volcano's last major eruption was 640,000 years ago. No one knows when it might erupt again, but geologists are watching the volcano closely. They are looking for warning signs that will tell them when Yellowstone is getting ready to erupt again.

above. Sometimes the magma rises all the way up to the surface. When magma erupts from a volcano, it becomes lava.

The Core

As you continue drilling, you leave the mantle. You reach the innermost layer of Earth. This is known as the core. The core makes up the last 2,166 miles (3,486 km) of your journey. The core is a hot, dense ball of iron and nickel at the center of the earth. The outer core is so hot that the rock and metal are liquid. The inner core is even hotter, but the rock here is solid. This may seem surprising since most materials melt as they get

Yellowstone's incredible geysers are powered by the volcanic forces at work beneath the park.

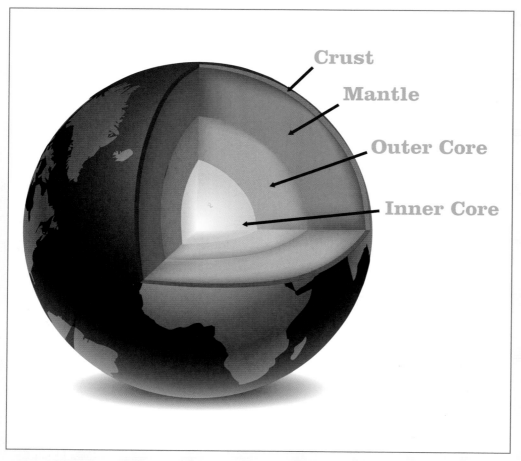

Crust
Mantle
Outer Core
Inner Core

The Earth's Layers
This diagram shows the layers that make up the earth. After reading about these layers, what did you imagine they looked like? How have your ideas changed? How does seeing the layers help you better understand the earth?

hotter. The reason the rocks are solid is the weight of all the rocks above. The pressure is so enormous that the rocks cannot melt.

Studying Earth's Layers

As exciting as a journey through the earth seems, no one has ever done it. So how do we know what Earth's inside looks like? A big clue comes from earthquakes. Earthquakes send waves of energy through the earth's layers. These waves of energy are called seismic waves. Scientists use a seismometer to listen to the waves.

When you knock on metal, it sounds different than when you knock on rock. The same

Magnetic Core

If you have ever used a compass, you know that the needle always points north. A compass works because Earth is a giant magnet. The compass needle is controlled by Earth's huge magnetic field. One end of the needle always points toward the North Pole, and the other end points toward the South Pole. Why is the earth magnetic? Scientists think it starts deep inside the earth. Earth's core is made of magnetic iron. Liquid iron is in the outer core. As the earth spins, the liquid rock rotates. This moving iron creates a giant magnetic field.

Seismometers create seismographs. These tell scientists how strong earthquakes are. The straight lines on the right of this seismograph show a decline in activity.

thing happens when seismic waves pass through the earth's layers. The waves travel at different speeds depending on what material they are going through. By listening to these waves, scientists can learn what makes up the earth's interior.

People have never reached the earth's mantle. But scientists have explored the possibility of drilling to the mantle on the ocean floor, where the crust is only four miles (6.4 km) thick. This excerpt describes why reaching the mantle is important:

> *Between Earth's molten core and hard, thin crust, the roughly 2,000-mile-thick (3,200-kilometer-thick) mantle contains the vast bulk of Earth's rocks. But we don't know much about them, because all we have are bits that have come to the surface via volcanoes or been trapped in ancient mountain belts.*
>
> *But all these mantle samples no longer really represent mantle conditions and makeup, since they've been altered in the long process of coming to the surface, so they [provide] only tantalizing glimpses of what lies below, scientists say.*
>
> Source: Richard A. Lovett. *"Scientists to Drill Earth's Mantle, Retrieve First Sample?"* National Geographic Daily News. *National Geographic Society, March 23, 2011. Web. Accessed November 27, 2013.*

Back It Up

The author of this passage is using evidence to support a point. Write a paragraph describing the point the author is making. Then write down two pieces of evidence the author uses to make the point.

CHAPTER THREE

HOW EARTH'S ROCKS ARE FORMED

From the mantle to the crust to the highest mountain, rocks are the most abundant material on Earth. Most rocks begin their lives deep within the earth. But different kinds of rock are formed in different ways.

Igneous Rocks

Most rocks begin as igneous rocks. These rocks are formed from the glowing, scorching liquid known as

Igneous rocks are formed from hardened lava and magma.

Underwater Giant

Earth is covered in volcanoes. But if you want to climb Earth's largest volcano, you'll need scuba gear. The world's largest volcano, called Tamu Massif, sits on the bottom of the Pacific Ocean. It is about the size of New Mexico. That is much bigger than the largest active land volcano, Hawaii's Mauna Loa. What would happen if Tamu Massif erupted? Don't worry— it last erupted 145 million years ago. Scientists believe it is extinct.

magma. Most magma forms in the upper mantle. Sometimes this magma oozes all the way to the surface, forming a volcano. When magma reaches the surface, it is called lava. As the lava cools it hardens into igneous rocks. Obsidian, basalt, and pumice are examples of igneous rock.

Sometimes magma rises but does not quite break through the surface. Instead it cools and hardens under the ground. Granite is an example of this kind of igneous rock. Over time, erosion and weathering may expose the granite. Erosion is the process by which rock and soil are broken down and moved somewhere

Granite, an igneous rock, makes up Mount Rushmore, where the faces of four US presidents are carved.

Old Rocks

Earth formed when a swirl of dust, rocks, and gas circling the sun turned into the planets of our solar system. Scientists think Earth is approximately 4.6 billion years old. The oldest rocks ever discovered from Earth are approximately 4 billion years old. They are also very rare. If Earth is so old, why aren't there more old rocks around? Blame the rock cycle. The planet is constantly recycling rocks. That means there are hardly any rocks left from Earth's early years. The oldest rock on Earth wasn't even made here. It is a meteorite from space. This meteorite was found in northwest Africa. Scientists believe it is more than 4.5 billion years old!

else. Weathering is the breaking down of natural features by wind and water. Weathering and erosion can cause igneous rocks to become sedimentary rocks. Heat and pressure cause igneous rocks to become metamorphic rocks.

Metamorphic Rocks

When an igneous or sedimentary rock is heated or squeezed, it can turn into metamorphic rock. This happens when tremendous heat and pressure result in the formation of new minerals

If you look at a metamorphic rock, such as gneiss, closely, you may be able to see squashed mineral grains and bent layers.

in a rock. The new metamorphic rock may look very different from the parent rock. This type of change is similar to putting unpopped kernels in a popcorn popper. The heat of the popper causes the kernels to change. After the kernels are popped, they have a different composition and appearance than the unpopped kernels.

Metamorphic rock does not melt, but the atoms and molecules are rearranged. One way metamorphic rocks form is from hot magma under the earth's surface. The heat from the magma bakes the nearby rocks. These rocks change into metamorphic rocks. Another way metamorphic rocks form is when plates collide and squeeze the land to form mountains. The pressure crushes the rocks, changing them into new rocks.

Metamorphism takes place under enormous heat or pressure. For that reason, metamorphic rocks tend to be very tough. Metamorphism can cause amazing changes in rocks. Gritty sandstone can change into hard quartzite. Soft mudstone can transform into flaky slate. Powdery limestone can become beautiful marble.

Sedimentary Rocks

Metamorphic rocks may be tough, but that doesn't mean they are safe from changing again. If metamorphic rock melts back into magma, it

Shale, a kind of sedimentary rock, is made mostly of compressed mud.

might become igneous rock. If metamorphic rock erodes into sediment or loose rock particles, it might become sedimentary rock. Have you ever noticed layers of rock in a cliff? Or maybe you've seen layers of rock where a hill has been cut away to make room for a road. These layers are the beginning of sedimentary rocks.

Rock layers form when crushed rock, or sediment, settles to the bottom of oceans, lakes, or rivers. As

Examining a piece of limestone, a sedimentary rock, may reveal the fossils of ancient sea creatures.

the layers pile up, the sediment is buried deeper and deeper. The pressure builds up. Over millions of years, the layers of rock get stuck together into a new kind of rock. This rock is called sedimentary rock. Shale is a kind of sedimentary rock formed from mud. Sandstone is made from bits of sand stuck together.

Some sedimentary rocks are the remains of living things. Limestone is made from crushed coral and seashells. As these living things die, their remains build up and get pressed together. Sedimentary rocks often contain fossils. These are the remains of living things turned to stone. Sedimentary rocks give scientists important clues for understanding Earth's past.

FURTHER EVIDENCE

Chapter Three discusses how different types of rocks are formed. What was one of the chapter's main points? What are some pieces of evidence in the chapter that support this main point? Check out the website at the link below. Does the information on this website support a main point in this chapter? Write a few sentences using new information from the website as evidence to support the information in this chapter.

How Rocks Are Formed
www.mycorelibrary.com/the-rock-cycle

THE DYNAMIC EARTH

Earth's rocks are continually being made, destroyed, and made again. Imagine one rock moving through the cycle. First, magma bubbles to the surface of the earth. It cools and forms igneous rock. As the years pass, the igneous rock is worn away by water and wind. The bits may be washed into the sea. Over millions of years, the layers get compacted into sedimentary rock.

Millions of years of weathering and erosion formed the stone arches of Arches National Park in Utah.

Pangaea

If you look at a globe, you will see continents surrounded by oceans. You may think the continents have always looked that way. Scientists once thought so too. In the early 1900s, German scientist Alfred Wegener proposed that Africa and South America once fit together. Fossils on the coast of Africa were identical to fossils on the coast of South America. Rock features, such as mountain ranges, on the two continents also matched. Wegener thought that all the continents fit together like a jigsaw puzzle. The continents had once been joined together. He called this ancient land *Pangaea*, which is Greek for "all lands."

With enough heat and pressure, the sedimentary rocks transform into metamorphic rock.

This is just one way a rock can move through the rock cycle. In the rock cycle, any kind of rock can be turned into any other kind of rock. Sedimentary rock can be made from pieces of igneous or metamorphic rock. Metamorphic rock can be formed when igneous or sedimentary rock is baked and squeezed. And any kind of rock can also get swallowed back into the earth. The rock can melt back into magma deep underground. One day it might bubble to the surface and form a new rock.

Moving Earth

Plate tectonics help keep the process of rock recycling going. According to the plate tectonics theory, the earth's crust is divided into huge plates. These plates move over time. Have you ever broken a ceramic plate and glued the pieces back together? This is what Earth's crust looks like. The ground beneath your feet may seem solid and still, but it's not. The crust is broken into pieces, and these pieces move.

Earth's plates are huge. Some have oceans on them. Some have an entire continent on them. The plates float on top of the soft, moving rock in the mantle. When the plates move, they bring the continents and oceans with them. Today, North and South America are drifting away from Europe and Africa. The movement is very slow, moving the continents apart approximately two inches (5 cm) per year. That is slower than your fingernails grow!

A scuba diver explores the widening gap between the North American and Eurasian tectonic plates.

How do scientists know where two plates meet? Earthquakes, volcanoes, and mountains reveal a lot. Earthquakes tell us where two plates are rubbing against one another. Volcanoes are places where magma erupts out of the mantle. Along some plate boundaries, long chains of volcanoes occur.

Plate Movements

Sometimes two plates carrying continents push against one another. These are called convergent plate boundaries. The land buckles and folds, forming mountains. This is how the Himalayan Mountains that separate India from the rest of Asia formed. Earthquakes are common along convergent boundaries.

At other convergent boundaries, plates moving toward each other do not crunch together. Instead one plate slides underneath the other. This is called a subduction zone. These are most common where two oceanic plates meet. These zones can also form when oceanic plates meet continental plates.

Volcanoes often form along subduction zones. In fact, subduction zones have the most violent earthquakes and volcanic eruptions of any plate boundary.

Sometimes two plates pull apart. These are divergent boundaries. Many of these boundaries are on the ocean floor. As the plates pull apart, magma rises through the gap in the ocean floor. The magma cools and hardens to form brand-new mountains. These mountain ranges are called mid-ocean ridges.

Other plates slide past one another. These are transform boundaries. Earthquakes are common at transform boundaries. The crust cracks and

Mount Everest

Mount Everest is the world's tallest mountain. It is part of the Himalayan mountain range. The two tectonic plates separating India and Asia collided approximately 50 million years ago. The Himalayas began forming approximately 30 million years ago. Today, these plates continue crunching together. The collision is pushing Mount Everest a few inches to the northeast every year. It is also causing Everest to grow taller by about 0.1 inches (2.5 mm) each year.

Mount Everest of the Himalayan mountains is gradually being pushed higher by the converging and folding plates below it.

breaks as it moves. But crust is not created or destroyed at transform boundaries.

Weathering and Erosion

Moving plates shape Earth in dramatic ways. Another powerful force for change is weather. When rocks sit outside, they begin to break down. Harsh weather, such as wind, rain, and snow, causes rocks to break down even faster.

Winds and crashing waves have weathered these rocks into unique shapes.

Sometimes rain beats down on a rock and dissolves bits of the rock. The water may trickle into a crack and freeze. As the water freezes, it pushes outward and cracks the rock. Sometimes plants grow on the rocks and break them apart. These changes are weathering.

Sometimes the weathered bits and pieces erode. Particles of rock may be blown away by wind or washed away by water. These particles may wash into a stream, river, ocean, or lake. Now the particles are called sediment. The sediment eventually settles to the bottom. With enough pressure, it will become sedimentary rock. Together, weathering and erosion shape the earth. They turn jagged rocks smooth. They wear down tall, jagged mountains into low, rounded ones. They carve landforms into cliffs and caves.

The earth is always changing. Weathering, erosion, and plate tectonics keep the rock cycle going. New rocks form as other rocks are eroded away. The rock cycle has helped give Earth the varied landscape it has today.

EXPLORE ONLINE

Chapter Four focuses on how plate tectonics and weathering keep the rock cycle going. The website below also has information about plate tectonics and the rock cycle. As you know, every source is different. What are the similarities between Chapter Four and the information you found on the website? Are there any differences? What can you learn from this website?

The Rock Cycle
www.mycorelibrary.com/the-rock-cycle

Weathering Rocks

Want to see with your own eyes what weathering can do to rocks? Shape a piece of modeling clay into a round ball. Wet the outside of the ball. Then wrap it with plastic wrap. Place the ball in the freezer overnight. Take the ball out the next morning and examine it closely. What do you see? Write a journal entry about how you did the experiment and what you learned about weathering.

Over time, freezing and thawing of rocks can cause them to break down.

Build Your Own Metamorphic Rock

Unwrap three pieces of soft candy, such as taffy or marshmallows. Don't eat them! Instead, stack the candy on a piece of waxed paper. Put one piece of candy on top of another. Then draw a picture of what your candy looks like. Put another piece of waxed paper over the top and press down. Peel off the waxed paper. What happened? Draw a picture of what the candy looks like after you squeezed it.

How is your candy similar to this metamorphic rock? Does it look like the picture you drew?

Heavy rain and snow caused this landslide in Washington State.

Erosion in Action

Over millions of years, erosion has shaped the earth. To see erosion in action, put some damp sand in a shallow dish. Shape the sand into a tiny mountain. Sprinkle the mountain with water from a watering can. What happens? Look for streams, lakes, and landslides to form. Where do the particles of sand go? Next, see what happens if you blow on the mountain through a straw.

Take a Stand

Chapter Four discusses the idea that Earth's continents have shifted. Do you think scientists can prove the continents have shifted? Or does this theory need more information? Write a short essay explaining your opinion. Make sure to give reasons for your opinion, as well as facts and details that support those reasons.

Tell the Tale

Chapter Two discusses an imaginary journey to the center of the earth. Write 200 words that tell the story of your journey into the earth. Describe the sights and sounds as you move through the earth. What is happening to the rock at each layer? What might you be worried about? Be sure to set the scene, develop a sequence of events, and write a conclusion.

Say What?

Studying the rock cycle can mean learning a lot of new vocabulary. Find five words in this book that you have never seen or heard before. Use a dictionary to find out what they mean. Then write the meanings in your own words, and use each word in a sentence.

Surprise Me

Chapter Four discusses some of the ways that Earth is changing. After reading this book, what two or three facts about the changing Earth did you find most surprising? Write a few sentences about each fact. Why did you find them surprising?

GLOSSARY

core
the central part of the earth

crater
a bowl-shaped valley around the opening of a volcano

crust
the outer layer of the earth

element
the simplest possible form of a substance

erosion
the process of being carried away by the action of water, wind, or glacial ice

lava
melted rock once it reaches the earth's surface

magma
melted rock material within the earth

mantle
the portion of the earth lying between the crust and the core

mineral
a solid chemical element or compound that occurs naturally from nonliving matter

sediment
materials deposited by water, wind, or glaciers

weathering
to change by exposure to the weather

LEARN MORE

Books

Korb, Rena. *Radical Rocks*. Edina, MN: Magic
    Wagon, 2008.

Tomecek, Steve. *National Geographic Kids:
    Everything Rocks and Minerals*. Washington, DC:
    National Geographic Children's Books, 2011.

Websites

To learn more about Rocks and Minerals, visit
booklinks.abdopublishing.com. These links are
routinely monitored and updated to provide the most
current information available.

Visit **www.mycorelibrary.com** for free additional tools
for teachers and students.

INDEX

ABOUT THE AUTHOR

Rebecca E. Hirsch is a former scientist and the author of dozens of books on science and nature for young readers. She lives in Pennsylvania with her husband, three children, one cat, and a small flock of chickens.